DK READERS

BEGINNING
1
TO READ

STAR WARS

Tatooine Adventures

Clare Hibbert

Come and explore the planet Tatooine (TA-TOO-EEN) and meet the many different creatures that live here.

This dry, desert world is far away, on the edge of the galaxy.

Two suns keep the planet very hot.

Planet

This is Anakin Skywalker.
He is a slave who
lives on Tatooine.

He belongs to a
junk merchant
called Watto.

Watto

Anakin fixes
machines for
Watto.

He builds a
droid called
C-3PO.

C-3PO will
be covered in
golden metal.

Droid

Anakin lives in
a busy city called
Mos Espa.

Domed roof

Many of the buildings in
Mos Espa have domed roofs.

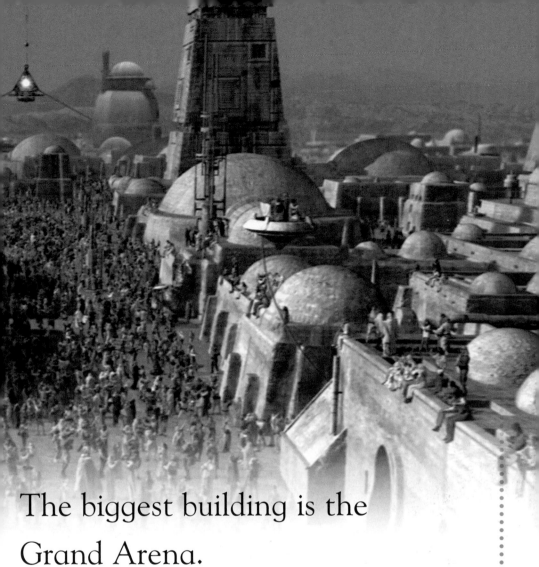

The biggest building is the
Grand Arena.

It has a famous racetrack.

Podracing is the most popular sport on Tatooine.

The Podracers go super-fast.

Anakin is racing. Go, Anakin, go! Some of the other creatures in the Podrace cheat, but they can't beat Anakin!

Sand People live on Tatooine.
They are also called Tusken Raiders.

They live in small camps far out
in the desert.

The Sand People are
fierce fighters.

Tusken Raiders ride across the sand dunes on big hairy beasts called banthas.

Banthas have shaggy coats
and long, curled horns.

They can survive for weeks
without water.

These little aliens are Jawas.
They are scavengers who buy
and sell things.

Jawas wear hooded brown cloaks.
All you can see are their eyes
that glow orange or yellow.

Scavenger

Wow! Look at this old hunk.
It's called a sandcrawler.

Jawas live inside sandcrawlers.
They drive them across the desert.

They stop to pick up scrap metal and machine parts to fix and sell.

The Jawas have found a droid called R2-D2.

Anakin has a son called Luke.
Luke grows up on Tatooine.
He is raised by the Lars family.
They have a moisture farm.
They collect water from the air.

_____Owen Lars

The Lars live
in the desert.
The nearest city
is Mos Eisley
(MOSS IZE-LEE).

Moisture farm

Beru Lars

This bar is in Mos Eisley.
It is full of troublemakers.

Luke is here to find someone
to fly him and his friends to
the planet Alderaan.

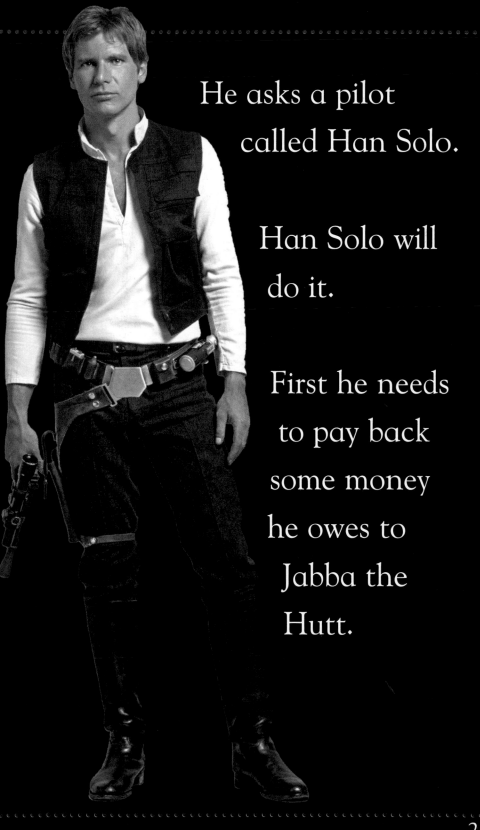

He asks a pilot
called Han Solo.

Han Solo will
do it.

First he needs
to pay back
some money
he owes to
Jabba the
Hutt.

Is this a giant slug?
No, it's Jabba the Hutt.
He's the most powerful being
on Tatooine.

Jabba is a crime lord.
He loves to make bets and
gamble money.
He has a terrible temper.

Jabba is protected by green-skinned guards.

They are strong, but not very smart.

The guards come from a
planet called Gamorr.
They have horns, tusks
and short, pig-like snouts.

Look out, C-3PO!
He's behind you!

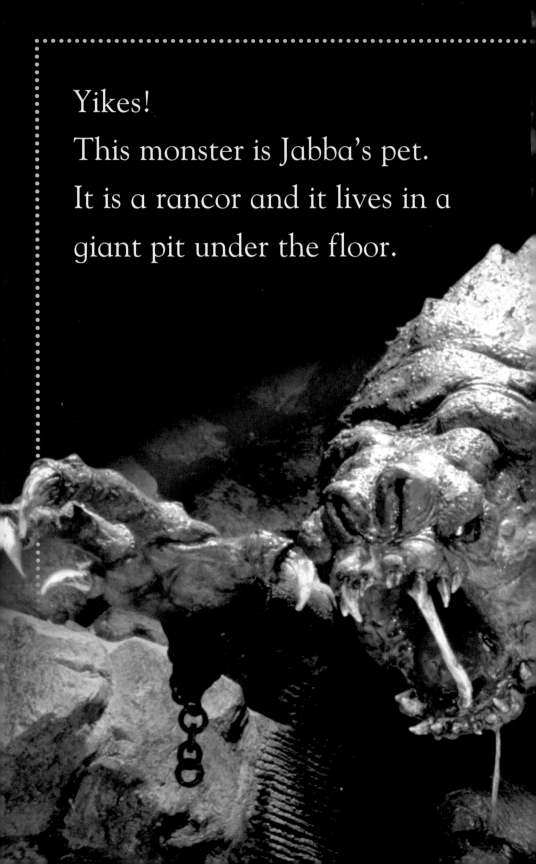

Yikes!

This monster is Jabba's pet.

It is a rancor and it lives in a

giant pit under the floor.

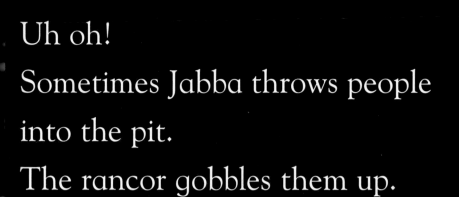

Uh oh!
Sometimes Jabba throws people
into the pit.
The rancor gobbles them up.

Fire! Fire!

Jabba the Hutt's sail barge has been blasted by a laser cannon. It's the end for you, Jabba.

You won't be cruising across the planet in this barge again. Looks like it's time for us to leave Tatooine!

Glossary

Droid
a robot

Domed roof
a roof that is shaped like half a ball

Moisture farm
a place where people collect water from the air

Planet
a ball of rock and gas that orbits around a star

Scavenger
someone who collects scrap and bits of metal